God Knows My Name

Joanne Dwyer Welihan

In Christ Jesus
Preschool

Benziger Publishing Company
Mission Hills, California

Special Editorial Consultant:
Irene H. Murphy

Illustrations:
Terry Anderson, Rosemary Deasy, Catherine Leary, Kathy McCarthy, Susan Nethery

Photography:
Steve McBrady, Dan Welihan

Nihil Obstat:
Sr. Christopher Smetanka, S.N.D.
Censor Deputatus

Imprimatur:
†Roger M. Mahony
Archbishop of Los Angeles
July 13, 1987

The nihil obstat and imprimatur are official declarations that a book or pamphlet is free of doctrinal or moral error. No implication is contained therein that those who have granted the nihil obstat and imprimatur agree with the contents, opinions, or statements expressed.

Send all inquiries to:
Benziger Publishing Company
15319 Chatsworth Street
Mission Hills, California 91345

Printed in the United States of America

ISBN 0-02-660040-4 (Student Text)
ISBN 0-02-660050-1 (Teacher's Edition)
ISBN 0-02-660060-9 (Teacher's Resource Kit)
     4 5 6 7 8 9   91 90

Contents

Part Four
I Like to Be Me

Special Days **61**

Part One

God Is Wonderful

Sing a new song to God.
Tell everyone how great God is!
Let everything on earth shout with joy—
    the sea, the flat land, all the trees of the forest.
God takes care of the world and everyone forever.

Adapted from Psalm 96

1 God Knows My Name

My Name

2 God Gives Us Everything

My Book

← Fold

God Made Everything

God Made Me

8.

1.

→ Cut

6.

3.

↑ Cut

9

← Fold

2.

7.

←cut

4.

5.

←cut

3 God Is Here

Still There

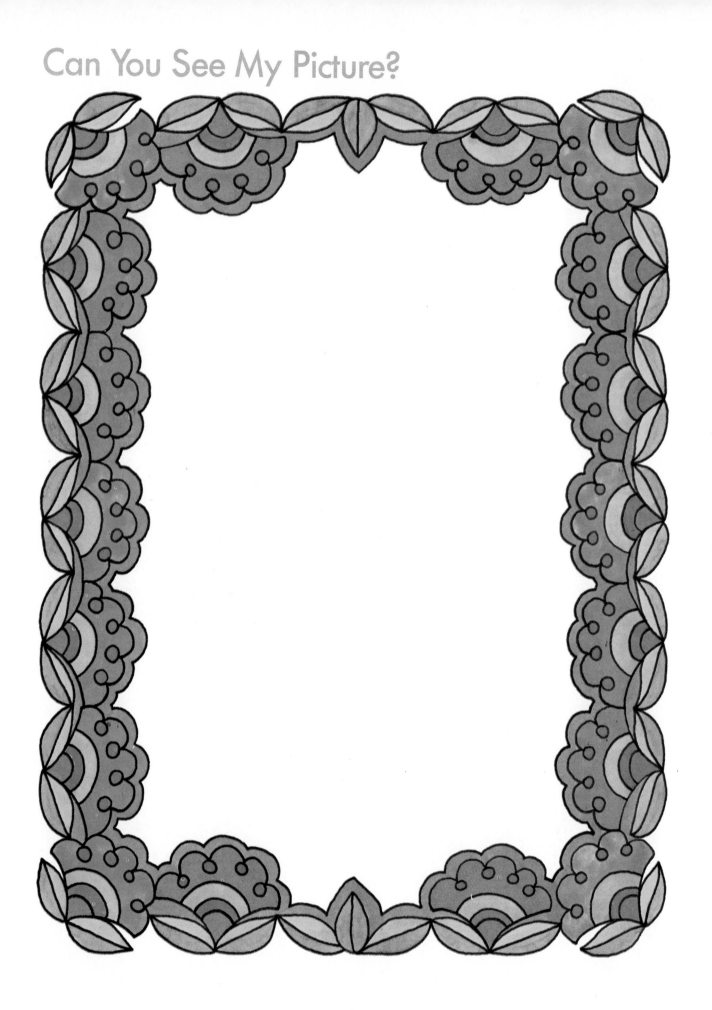

4 God Always Loves Me

Pinocchio

Gepetto makes a puppet named Pinocchio. Gepetto loves Pinocchio.

Gepetto buys him new clothes and books for school.

Pinocchio goes to a puppet show instead of to school.

Pinocchio sees he is turning into a donkey.

Pinocchio saves Gepetto's life.

Pinocchio becomes a real boy at last!

My Puppet

5 Where Do Things Come From?

Getting Food Ready to Eat

God Gives Us What We Need

6 Where Do Things Go?

Some Things Change

What to Wear?

Part Two

Gifts of God's World

Give thanks to God.
God is always kind.
God made the land and seas.
God is always kind.
God made the great lights of the sun, the moon, the stars.
God is always kind.
God, who is so strong, always helps us.
God is always kind.

Adapted from Psalm 136

7 God's World Is Light and Dark

Day and Night

Which Light Is Right?

8 God's World Is All Colors

Some Colors Keep Us Safe

Red, yellow, green; what do the colors mean?
Red means stop. Green means go.
You must wait when you see yellow.

God's Colors

9 God's World Has Many Sounds

Which Make Sounds?

Can You Make These Sounds?

10 God's World Has Things to Feel

A Song about Things to Feel

Kittens are soft.

Sand feels scratchy.

Tree trunks feel rough.

Water is splashy.

Sunshine feels warm.

Snowballs are cold.

But love feels the best.

With a hand I can hold.

11 God's World Is Big and Little

Alice in Wonderland

Alice follows the White Rabbit.

Alice is too big to get through the little door.

Alice is so small she floats through a keyhole!

Alice is too big for the White Rabbit's house.

The flowers are bigger than Alice.

Alice has tea.

Big and Little

12 God's World Has Many Shapes

Find the Shapes

Find My Shadow

I Belong to a Family

Listen, I will tell you about God:
God is wonderful!
When I was a child, my family told me:
God is wonderful!
Now, I am grown up and I tell you, children:
God is wonderful!
When you are grown up, tell your children too:
God is wonderful!

Adapted from Psalm 78

34

Who Will Help?

17 I Make Mistakes

Peter Rabbit

The little rabbits go off to play.

Fresh vegetables taste so good!

Oh, oh, Peter!

A cold, wet hiding place.

Escape!

Poor Peter.

Peter's Escape

18 I'm Sorry

The Three Little Kittens

We've lost our mittens.

No pie for you.

We've found our mittens.

You shall have some pie.

Dressing for dinner.

Yummy.

Can You Find the Mittens?

Can You Find the Mittens?

Part Four
I Like to Be Me

Oh, God, you made every part of me!
You see everything that I do.
Oh, God, you have wonderfully made me.
Oh, God, you can always help me.
You have done more things than I can talk about.
You have done more things than there are grains of sand on
the beach.

Adapted from Psalm 139

19 I Like to Be Me

All about Me

This makes me happy.

This makes me sad.

More about Me

I do this best.

I like this best.

A Halloween

Halloween Maze

How Many Witches Can You Find?

Piñatas Are Fun

CUT HERE ↓   CUT HERE↓   CUT HERE↓

CUT

71

Holiday Senses

My favorite holiday thing to touch

My favorite holiday smell

CUT

FOLD

My favorite holiday sound

My favorite holiday thing to do

My favorite holiday sight

My favorite holiday taste

CUT

FOLD

74

Christmas Tree Ornaments

Valentine's Day

People I Love

My Valentine

I LOVE YOU

Valentine Cut-outs

The Selfish Giant

Playing in the garden is fun.

What a mean giant!

Winter would not go away.

Spring is back—almost.

The giant makes up for his meanness.

"The children are the most beautiful flowers of all."

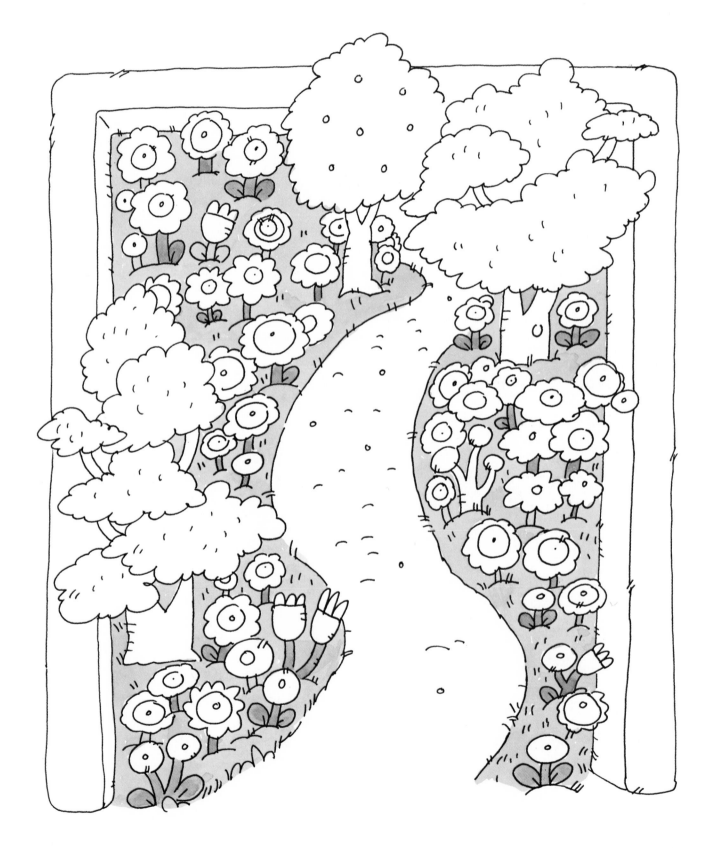

Easter Cards

CUT HERE

CUT HERE

83

Which Bunny Is Different?

Easter Maze

G My Birthday

How Old Are You?

Birthday Surprise

H Let's Pretend

What Am I Pretending?

Picture in the Clouds

Growing Up

The Three Little Pigs

One day three little pigs set off to see the world.

Two pigs at home.

A strong brick house.

"I'll huff and I'll puff . . ."

A smart pig.

The end of the wolf.

J Look What I Can Do!

What Am I Doing?

PLACE
CENTER DOT OF
SEE-SAW HERE

CUT ALONG DOTTED LINES

Seesaws Are ● for Sharing

How Can They Move?

I Can Do This!

Craft Pages

For Lesson 22

For Lesson A

For Lesson D

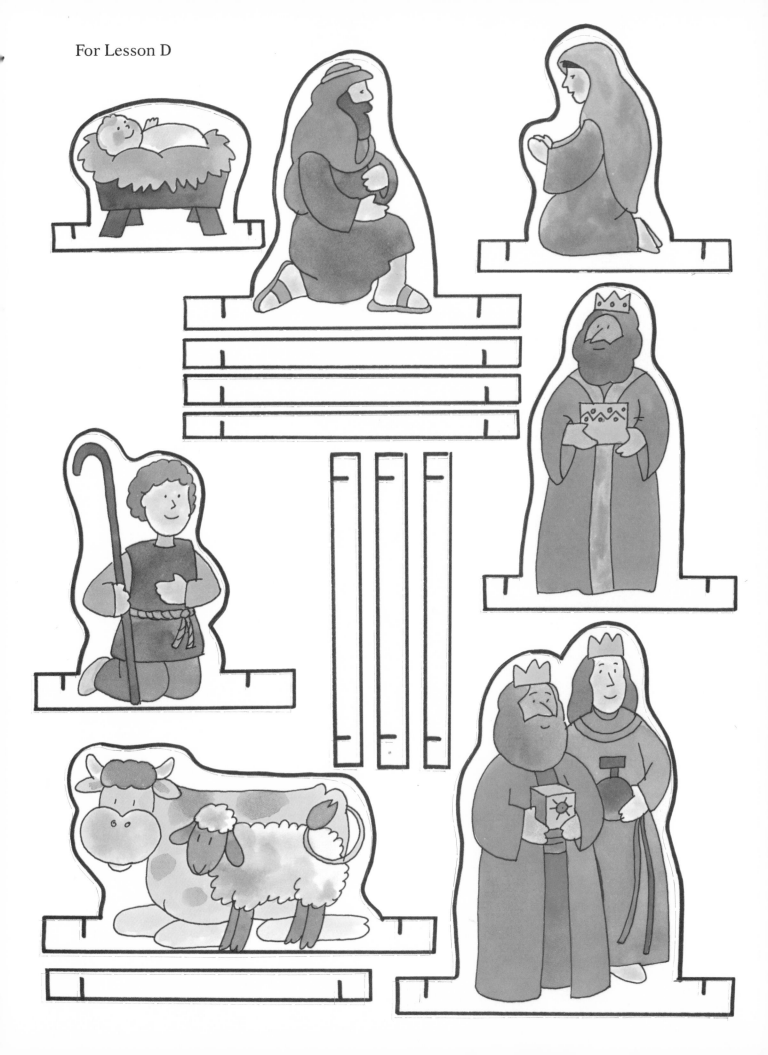